By Christopher Dow

Fiction
Effigy
    Book I: Stroud
    Book II: Oakdale
The Books of Bob
    Devil of a Time
    Jumping Jehovah
The Clay Guthrie Mysteries
    The Dead Detective
    Landscape with Beast
    The Texas Troll Unlimited
Roadkill
The Werewolf and Tide, and other Compulsions

Nonfiction
Lord of the Loincloth (nonfiction novel)
Book of Curiosities: Adventures in the Paranormal
Occasional Pilgrimage: Essays on Film, Literature, and Other Matters
Living the Story: The Meandering, True, and Sometimes Strange
    Adventures of an Unknown Writer
    Vol.I: Growing Up Takes a Long Time
    Vol. II: Growing Old Takes Longer

Martial Arts
The Wellspring: An Inquiry into the Nature of Chi
Circling the Square: Observations on the Dynamics of Tai Chi Chuan
Elements of Power: Essays on the Art and Practice of Tai Chi Chuan
Alchemy of Breath: An Introduction to Chi Kung
Leaves on the Wind: A Survey of Martial Arts Literature (Vol. I–VI)

Poetry
City of Dreams
The Trip Out
Texas White Line Fever
Networks
A Dilapidation of Machinery
Puzzle Pieces: Selected Poems

Editor
The Abby Stone: The Poetry of Bartholo Dias
The Best of Phosphene
The Best of Dialog

TEXAS WHITE LINE FEVER

TEXAS WHITE LINE FEVER

CHRISTOPHER DOW

Phosphene Publishing Company
Temple, Texas

Texas White Line Fever
© 2011 by Christopher Dow
ISBN 13: 978-0-9796968-7-9
ISBN 10: 0979696879

Published by
Phosphene Publishing Company Temple, Texas, U.S.A.
phosphenepublishing.com

All rights reserved. This book may not be reproduced, in whole or part, without permission from the publisher, except for the use of brief quotations in reviews, articles, or critical works.

Cover: "Rails: Lubbock County, Texas," by Tommy LaVergne

4.2

For Julie

CONTENTS

AGGREGATE VELOCITY
Clownish———17
I Knew You Were Coming———18
Moon on Water———19
Grackle Flight———20
In Between———21
Heisenberg———22
Non Sequitur———23
Flicker———24
Maze———25
Lifeboat———26
Fringe of the Storm———27
Sailing the Seven Seas———28
The Final Word Is Tattered———29
Zen Garden———30
Forest Path———32
Afternoon Air———33

SNIPS AND SNIPPETS
Shoes———39
Home Away From———40
Japan———41
Honesty———42
Lake———43
Weapons———44
Past Due———45
Epitaph II———46
Drugs———47
Editors———48
Formula———49
Tiptoes———50
Oracles———51
Dangerous People———52

Religious Wars———53
Time Takes———54
Shadows———55
The Window's Allure———56
Black Eye———57
The Breaths That Pass———58

OTHER PLACES
Facing West East———61
Dune———62
Near Four Corners———63
Outside Durango———64

PITH AND VINEGAR
Stuck in Hell———67
Cut-and-Paste Culture———68
Intelligent Design———69
Religion and Reality———70
Headless———71
Oil———72
People———73
Tough Man———74
Condolences———75
Give and Take———76
Paths———77
Desire———78
Game Face———79
Assassin———80
Her Spiders———81

EFFECTS AND DEFECTS
The Phenomenon of Being Alone in Crowds———85
The Art of Self-Hatred———86
Impediments———87

Tomorrow———88
The Acquisition of Confusion———89
Magnesium Dreams———90
Learning to Live in the Middle of a House Fire———93
Welcome, Traveler———94
Elegy for Scott———96

TEXAS WHITE LINE FEVER
Quick Change, Unexpected Beauty———101
Southeast Texas———102
Radio Towers———103
The Highway Rural———104
183———106
Forgotten Road———107
Cruise Control II———108
Valleys———109
Across Mustang Creek———110
Certainty———112
The High Chaparral———113
Seminole Canyon———114
Mess Box Creek———115
Light Is Sharp———116
White Lines———117
Westward———118

TEXAS WHITE LINE FEVER

AGGREGATE VELOCITY

Clownish

With a clown, you see through the actor,
Into a vague sense of self-consciousness.
He's not playing blindman's bluff, now:
He's playing for real.
While he's trying to restart his car
After he runs out of gas,
His battery goes dead.
It parses meaningfully
Because he knows how to kill
In more ways than there are to die.
You may be able to avoid all those,
But when he pulls compassion
From its secret holster
Beneath his harlequin patchwork
And aims it at your heart,
You know you're done for.

I Knew You Were Coming

I knew you were coming
Long before you did,
But didn't realize it.
I'd lived with the image
Of you for years
But didn't recognize it
Until the exact moment we met.
And in that moment we touched—
Sparked.

Moon on Water

The moon on the water
Played a storm song for the sole survivor
Of a series of unfortunate crossings—
Distracting rides across waves
Teach you things you might not
Want to know about yourself.

Grackle Flight

Something has excited the grackles.
They're rapidly flying in whole groups
From one side of the bayou to the other,
Swooping like swift, dark kites
Across the murky green water.
Most days, they hunt on both sides
Of the channel, also in large groups,
But in a more sedate and random fashion.
Yesterday, they flew across in a swift
Single file, urged on by one squawking
About a third of the way down the line.
But today, they're all squawking
As they seesaw back and forth across the water.
Perhaps there is a hawk unseen to my eyes
In the margin of the woods.
Perhaps today it is the grackles
Who are being hunted.

In Between

The world began at dawn,
Ended at sundown.
Before dawn, there was only void,
And everything we remember a dream.
After sundown, there will be only void,
And everything we will become a fantasy.

Heisenberg

If the act of observing
Changes the observed,
What of the stars?
Do we change them?
Do the inhabitants
Of their planets,
Seeing our feeble flicker,
Observe and thus change us?

Non Sequitur

There are occasions when
restructuring the current
in tandem with
areas of emphasis
is not for new designs.

If efforts focus on the audience,
recommend a review,
corrective actions,
and activity to clarify intent
in this age of hyperreality.

Distance goes around the circle,
guided by the discovery
that interpretation is not a game of dissent,
only something that was about to be born,
something that, in the end, was gone.

Then I think of shotguns and a shy albatross and wonder:
Am I going to be a grouchy old man, bewildered?

Flicker

Flicker across eyelid panorama,
Imp in and out of the bushes,
Every time a different hat.
Let me ride up across the sky,
Land on rooftops,
Cull wind in hands
And hair, and dance.
The courtyard spreads a carpet
Gold and rust beneath a broom
And sweeping steps.
Crystal in soft cloth.

Maze

Craven could easily stand for any
Reason why such fear came into being—
You just couldn't make an adventure of it.
Look at how you justify
A scandal revisited
That lurks in the dark corners
Of everyone's eyes.
Now close your eyes….

I've gone to grab the magic in the black castle
While you make your way into a maze
Of ill-dignified distance and headless forms,
Not realizing that there is no way out
Once you've given yourself to the minotaur.

My best advice:
Free play with an unconscious mind,
A strategy of Tinkertoys,
Insignificant divertissements,
A vocabulary for directions,
And children playing blindman's bluff.
My only advice:
Who's in charge depends on whose feet are on the ground,
And there's nowhere for a breathy elegy to look but up.

Lifeboat

Wait, they tell us
As we float adrift,
Seemingly becalmed
And surrounded by the mists
Of uncertain horizons.
Wait for the moment.
Wait for the time.
Wait for the future.
Waiting for the rhyme
To fit the rhythm of hearts
Already embarked upon
A voyage into mystery,
Hearts already riding an evening tide
From old, familiar ports
Where sailors doss among companions
Who do not smell of brine
Or of breezes blowing the scents
Of spices from islands beyond the mists.
As we sail our ship of two
Upon these troubled, darkened seas,
Let our love light us
And our small craft
Until the dawn breaks.

Fringe of the Storm

The dry spell had gone on long enough
That everything was dried up:
The lawn where the sun hit all day
And the leaves on the trees.
In the sudden cool wind
Cast off from the failing southwest
Fringes of a hurricane that came ashore
At the mouth of the Mississippi,
Leaves blew off and landed in the bayou.
For a long time afterward,
They floated there, a tiny armada
Of pale yellow sails
Wafted this way then that
By the wind as it gusted
Down the channel.

Sailing the Seven Seas

The experienced boatman,
The mysteries of water,
The arcana of channels
And hazards murky, obscure.
Unseen currents bear the craft
To exotic ports of call,
To verdant foreign deltas.

The Final Word Is Tattered

Playing is irresponsible for those
Who so richly deserve it:
Bullies, being masters
Of greed and desperation,
Use sleight of hand
And diminish themselves
Through pomp and circumstance.

Although no weapon was unleashed in anger,
The sides were clearly engaged in maneuvers
Violent
With possibilities of discovering
Remote representations of primitive processes.

A stable point, if there is one at all,
Is that people are always meeting people.
And it's not the end of the world
Though whole lives are ruled and ruined
By the whims of tyrants and terrorists.
So, my friend,
We shall be well departed
To a place where
We can still find excursions
Across oceanic boundaries,
Where the sheen of certainty
Is wiped clean by the hand of strange fate.

Zen Garden

Still yet implying movement.
Remote yet immediate.
Formalistic yet conjuring wild beauty.
Bounded, it encompasses the world.

The stones, never polished
But prized for their patina of ages,
Never cut but celebrated
For the uncultivated images they evoke.
The stones, placed just so in their settings
Of gravel, white sand, or water,
Emphasize natural harmony
With contrasts between
The smooth and rough,
The light and dark,
The delicate and harsh.
The stones in their settings
Isolate true and essential nature.

The meditative act of placing the stones
Or raking the sand.
Raking the sand into waves
Rippling outward like the energy of life.
Or is it inward to break
Against the base of mountains?
Austerity masking inner peace and joy.

Contemplated, it brings stillness
To the mind.
Cultivated, sweetness

To the soul.
Perhaps deeper stirrings
Resonate within.

Not a garden, but the face of nature's spirit
Animating a landscape in miniature.

Forest Path

There is no map
Of the forest of illusion,
The forest of learning.
But we cannot live
These illusions and learn
Without cutting trees
And making paths.

Where will this forest path lead you
After it emerges from the wild woodland,
Into the void beyond the tree line?
The correct path
Is cleared in advance.
It will take you to where your story ends.

Afternoon Air

The spirit of dogs
Is in the dry, breeze-blown leaf
As it skitters across the brick patio,
Beckoned at fall's command.

Far from torchlight's call—
Farther still before that damn monkey brain
Gives up its cavorting and posturing—
Trees speak the language
Of play with gestures
Of bravery, while trying to ignore
The winds and dry seasons.

After the quick winds of yesterday,
The air is still beneath the white noise
Of the hum and chirp of insects
Sliced by the semidistant roar
Of a jet airliner flung skyward
On a thrust of sound as tangible
As longing.

A loud, complex, unidentifiable clattering—
Or is it a swiftly moving firefight?—
Comes closer and louder
Then suddenly angles away
And disappears into
The general hubbub.
Turned a corner out of my life,
Without definition, without explanation,
Without knowing if it was
An incredible rattletrap of a junk car
Bravely holding together

Or the sounds of empire
Crumbling.

Sometimes the air is so still
That it encases in an aural nutshell
Everything in all directions.
Sometimes it blows in the distance
And this way or that.
Sometimes despair and joy begin
To look the same:
Different names for the spectrum
Of life's progression,
Directed by blind supposition
And sheer luck.
Sometimes I try to make sense
Of too much to make sense of.
And sometimes it all makes
Sense and nonsense at the same time.
Can we ever know the beyond
Before it has too quickly passed?

The large hawk
With the cream breast hunts.
It has targeted this area for weeks,
But this time, a squadron
Of blue jays chase it off
With machine-gun squawks
And darting beaks.
No free lunch anywhere, buddy.
Especially here.
Especially us.
As soon as the jays have escorted
The lonely predator out of sight,
Scores of other birds and a few squirrels
Come out to frolic and forage
In the cool, sunlit autumn air

Beneath the light canopy.
Most of the birds are migrants
And will fly with tomorrow's breeze.
The squirrels will remain
Until, hawk's prey, they, too,
Depart on some zephyr.

Southeast gusts begin to scrub treetops.
With contradictory winds,
The trees may be uncertain
As to how long they have
Before promised frigid temperatures
And heavier, more-prolonged pressures
From different directions
And colder dimensions
Begin to strip them
To spare autumnal beauty
That withers around the seed
Of another generation.
But, at last, as always,
The wind changes direction,
And its clean chill,
Stronger with each passing day,
Washes over my face,
Promising a release
From music that plays
Before its instruments make a sound.

SNIPS AND SNIPPETS

Shoes

A person's life is like shoes:
Plentiful when outgrown quickly,
Rarer when quickly worn out,
And receiving less wear
When the wearer is worn out.

Home Away From

Sometimes there's no place
I'd rather be than home,
And no place I'd rather go
Than away.

Japan
(3/11/2011)

No grounding. Water.
Half as many streets half-filled.
Sounds of clash and wail.

Honesty

A man willing to be honest
Is like a blind man willing to see.

Lake

From the air, the lake
Was long and narrow,
Bloating the slender river
Like a python's recent meal.

Weapons

Breasts so bound they perch
On her aggressive young chest
Like weapons of war.

Past Due

Knew it, blew it.
Had a chance,
But didn't do it.

Epitaph II

He stumbled onto the stage,
Mumbled a few lines,
Then staggered offstage.

Drugs

Never enough;
Always too much.

Editors

Editors edit
Because they are editors.
They might rearrange
Even a tanka about
An editing conference.

Formula

Cut down the grime,
Boost up the shine.

Tiptoes

Tiptoeing around.
Focus again as the world
Crosses its fingers.

Oracles

Older oracles
Have not fared well, turned into
Bland fortune cookies.

Dangerous People

All these dangerous
People walking around us.
Probably I'm one.

Religious Wars

Religious wars are
Like storm clouds obscuring stars'
Universal truths.

Time Takes

Time takes everything.
It even takes memory
Of the universe.

Winter Shadows

At this time of year,
The shadows remember
The cold rather
Than forget the heat.

The Window's Allure

The window's allure:
Cinematography of
The world going by.

Black Eye

Reality can hit you in the face,
Sneak up on you from behind,
Come out of left field,
Deal you a right hook,
Drop on your head
Or in your lap,
Shake your foundations.
Shake you at your core.

The Breaths That Pass

Do you pine for all those loves lost,
Or only the one, the love that lasts?
Do you mourn the breaths that pass,
Or only the one, that breath, the last?

OTHER PLACES

Facing West East

Facing west east of the Rockies.
Climbing over the toes of mountains.
Walking through a vale of lodgepole pines.
Slats of the stream below
Dance in the sunlight,
Water emitting bass notes as it tumbles
Through tumbled boulders.
My companion warns of ticks
That wait in ambush and leap
From the trees at the slightest shadow.
He was bit with the benign sort
Of Rocky Mountain fever
Thirty years ago and never left.

Dune

My face speaks in hieroglyphs
Written by the wind.
Every time it blows,
I change my mind.

Near Four Corners

1
Falling out of southwest Colorado,
Descending the wrinkled toe knuckles of mountains
Where houses cling precariously to hillsides.
As the terrain dries to northern New Mexico desert,
I am reminded of what a friend the pine tree is to mankind.
It helps tame the land,
It provides building materials for shelter,
It's so good at what it does,
So quick to replenish itself.
Adobe will prevail from here
To the jungles of Central America.
I will not see the end of it this journey.

2
Land of Enchantment,
The adobe hovel,
And the double-wide
Santa Fe-style mobile home.
Between Durango and Farmington,
Farmers water their fields.
Some use big circular sprayers,
Some long, wheeled contraptions carrying pipes
That roll across the fields
Like implacable armies on the march.
There is as yet no sun,
And it's early enough,
And it's cool enough
That their touch
Leaves circles and swaths
Of white rime on the dry brown earth—
Lacy enchantments that will vanish
Beneath the scrutiny of daybreak.

Outside Durango

The Animus River, strong, cold,
Waxes and wanes with the surge of snowmelt.
This far down from the highlands,
The swell comes at dusk.
At night, a cold wind blows down the valley.
There are too many things to know.
The rocky river banks, the origin of trees,
The startling blue sky that turns
Each night to black to reveal stark stars
And the ephemeral truths beyond their spacings.

A mist flows down the valley
On the heels of the wind.
Is gravity heaviest at the seams?
Think of a boat set free on a lake—
Even without a wind, it will drift to shore.
Think of fault lines, think of a road
And endless travel.
The seam is the interface
Where one thing becomes another,
Where chaos lives for a moment
In the confusion between
This and that, here and there,
Then and now.
Can we truly journey to other realms
Over bridges of uncertainty?

PITH AND VINEGAR

Stuck in Hell

Stuck in Hell.
There's the light.
Up there.
Here's my ball and chain.

At a party
Football in my eyes,
Rap in my ears,
Dogs all around
Begging for attention.

Where's the darkness?

Cut-and-Paste Culture

You take a snippet from this,
A tad from that,
Bootleg some music,
Bootleg some images,
Show some tits and ass,
Mix it all up
With a lot of sly references
To the ghosts of media past,
Hope it goes viral.
It may not be original,
It may not mean anything,
But isn't it funny?
Isn't it cool?
Isn't it weird?
Isn't it outrageous?
Isn't it?

Intelligent Design

I give you the two weakest joints
Holding the weight of the entire body.
I give you a head too large
For its spindly neck or the birth canal.
I give you the appendix—
Without citation.
I give you birth defects
And clogged arteries
And stroke and Alzheimer's.
I give you warts.
I give you ligaments that separate,
And cataracts, and arthritis, and constipation.
I give you aging.
And I give you the human brain,
Filled with ignorance and deception,
Primed for destruction,
Verging on madness.

God works in such mysterious ways
That even he is baffled
By his own incompetence,
Lack of engineering skills,
And failure of foresight.

Religion and Reality

Fuck you, God,
And Devil, too.
I want nothing to do
With either of you.
All I can hope
Is the materialists are right,
And oblivion's the end
Of man's sorry plight.

Headless

When John Kennedy was shot,
The country lost its head.
Now we're run by greedy guts
And military butts instead.

Oil

Life obviously
    has a spiritual component
    of some sort.
Think of oil.
    Not the politics
    or economics
    or even the chemistry.
Think about how oil is all that remains
    of the physical bodies
    of vast quantities of life.
But something that once was there
    —the animating force—
    no longer is.
If life were as simple as chemicals,
    then all that primordial soup
    of the essence of mass quantities of life
    might get up and start oozing around
    all over the place of its own volition.
    And motive.
Like the Blob,
    it might inundate us all,
    suck us in,
    digest us with its toxic juices
    to feed its own temporal needs.

People

The seething mind of America,
Splashed in glory across our home screens.
Sickness eating like worms
Through our culture, our society,
Our minds. We've gone
From being the land of the greatest producers
To that of the greatest consumers,
To that of the greatest wasters,
Scorning the idea of a progress
That once made us great.

Too many people!
Too many people!
There are too many people!
The Ganges running like an open sore,
Seas cluttered with plastic,
Chernobyl and Fukushima spewing nuclear toxicity
For miles. For generations.
Is this where we're going as a race:
Wallowing in our own excesses,
Creating our own wastelands,
Reeking of self-annihilation,
Consuming ersatz pabulum
And the detritus of our own excrement?

Tough Man

He's rough! He's tough!
He's Tough Man—the one man
Rugged enough for anything.

Funny thing is, sometimes
He doesn't feel all that tough.

But he is! Real tough!
Tough as tree bark,
Tough as nails,
Tough as the insides
Of a politician's soul.

Tough Man ain't got no
Sissy, sensitive side.
He can take anything—
Even stuff that would make
Mickey Rourke cry.

Condolences

I'm so sorry.
I'm sorry for your loss.
It comes to all of us.

He was a great man.
He lived life to the hilt.
Look at all he built.

He's in a better place.
He's at peace, now.
He's taken his final bow.

He's not in pain—
Better than those last days.
The Lord is mysterious in all His ways.

I forgive you.

Give and Take

It is impossible to assume
That a relationship
Is an assertion of the latest
Need to identify
The various dimensions
Of universal possibilities.
It might be just a cover-up.

Paths

The path is not down
On any map.
True places never are.
I wanted to travel it,
But you just wouldn't
Go that far.

Desire

Desire is a porcelain angel
As blushing as hot marble.
She pictures time
As a slow ocean
And dances like
A liquid ghost
After those who
Bleed perfumes
Of steely fire
And dazzling air.

Game Face

Tired of putting on a game face
When I don't feel all that game.
Sometimes I feel like a bundle
Of nerves with skin on it.

Now say that in a thick East Texas drawl.

Assassin

I'm going to kill you.
Sorry to be so literal.
I used to value metaphor
And obscure references,
But time has treated me cruelly,
And I cannot recall
That frame of mind.
So here is the bullet you forged,
Here is the gun you provided,
And here is the end.

Her Spiders

There are fifty plastic spiders in a bottle.
She's one of them.
She's the leader.
Pretty soon, she's going to open the bottle,
And they'll all come alive,
And she'll lead them out.

Just kidding.
She isn't one of the spiders.
She's the person holding the bottle.
She's going to open it
And pour the plastic spiders down your neck.

Then they'll come alive.

EFFECTS AND DEFECTS

The Phenomenon of Being Alone in Crowds

A crowd is the ultimate pluralism.
Aloneness is not necessarily loneliness.
Displacement is the true loneliness.

People sit at the same table,
Immersed in the smells of food and acquaintanceship,
And don't acknowledge the sharing.

The voices that rise above the rest.
Sitting in this seat among all the seats.
Looking at the faces.

I accidentally replicated a computer file a dozen times.
Without a second thought,
I deleted all but a single copy.

The Art of Self-Hatred

Purpose
Grief is unnecessary prelude
To a change of implications
Said to have existed since the Bronze Age.

Preparation
Endorse a structure of oblique extension and evolution
Built upon a foundation of years of deep reflection that,
Had that same attention been more well directed,
Might have granted time for further reflection.

Process
Initiating multidimensional discursive
Digressions from perspective,
Performing change like a surgical procedure,
Evaluating the influence of the unclear,
Assuming the assimilation,
Accumulating and divesting playfully,
Fighting the real enemies before it's too late,
Fanning the flames so when hard times come knocking,
Reason will rule out accumulated coherence.

Reward
To people used to eating shit,
Everything tastes like shit,
And finished is an optimistic word.

Impediments

There are impediments to understanding.
Machines break down.
Reality breaks down
But is somehow rebuilt
Though we can never know
Both velocity and position of an object.
How can we tell the difference
Between asymmetry and complexity?
How will we be able to measure the distinction
Between essence and existence
When the villagers are at Frankenstein's gate?

Tomorrow

I live with a yardful of dogs,
And every time I sit outside
And look around,
Some asshole's looking back at me,
Taking a dump.
Pretty much the same everywhere
In this shitty town,
Where everyone is killing
The world for ease and profit
And a slice of a paradise
That won't be there
Tomorrow.

While America dreams
A deep and dreamless sleep,
Its unkillable hospital germs crawl
Across surfaces shiny with pain,
Burnished by grief,
And hung with pastoral paintings
Of places patients and their families
Most definitely would rather be
Instead of dreading
The paradise that probably will arrive
Tomorrow.

Tomorrow, you assholes.
Tomorrow, you germs.
Just you wait and see.

The Acquisition of Confusion

It's sometimes pretty difficult to tell
Whether you're dealing with compound strategies
Or designations of voluntary service
While serving as an agent
Of the permutations of expression.
Does that explain why an individual speaks
To the universal image?
A study on the acquisition of confusion
Suggests that the image shows us
The world of things in space,
That relation is how we distinguish
Different realms of being from one another.
We are all adults in this thumbnail photo
Of our sojourn for an hour upon
The deck of the Marie Celeste.

Magnesium Dreams

1
The arrogant Chinese girl
With an American accent
Insisted on rearranging my desk
Before she would teach me
The new computer application.
I petulantly refused to let her
And placed the writing pad where I wanted
And deliberately moved the eighteenth-century book
For good measure.
She gave me a stern and scornful look.

2
A rock chasm opened beside the road
And a car bearing an innocent woman
Plunged into it.
I descended the rocky cliff face to rescue her
And found stone shelves adorned
With enough eyeglasses to stock an optometry store.
I rescued the woman and took her to a restaurant
Where my supervisor was wearing
A milky white bowl as a hat.
Above the bowl, attached to it by a spring,
Was an inverted saucer.
I complimented him on his new fashion
But remarked how peculiar it was.

3
She wanted to make love,
But the hardwood floor and tassled rug
Were slopped with chocolate pudding,
And the workers had to clean it up
By spooning it into saucers.
They ate some, too.

4
Inside the house of my father
That was not the house of my father,
We built a vehicle—
Was it a car or an airplane?—
Out of old vinyl rock-and-roll albums.
We knew it would take us far
And to the right places.
In the living room was a brand new pool table,
All clean green felt and shiny, polished dark wood.
Attached to its side was a rack
Bearing twenty cue sticks,
But we didn't want to play.
With me was Ray,
Looking exactly the same as he did
The last time I saw him forty years ago.

5
I was talking to a man
Who insisted he was my illegitimate older brother—
The production of a liaison between by father
And my mother's brother's wife.
He was twenty years my junior
And bore absolutely no resemblance
To either my father or my aunt,
So I thought his statement absurd,
Yet his force of conviction
Planted a seed of doubt in my mind.
Maybe he was my brother.

6
Waking:
Sometimes it's like turning on a light switch.
Sometimes it's like climbing out of a deep well
Or clawing upward through the earth of a fresh grave.
And sometimes, it's like being spit forth
From a vast, billowing darkness.

Learning to Live in the Middle of a House Fire

Insanity and spiritual songs
In the soul of the saint,
Intense with torn messages,
Who gave to Misery all he had
And suggested that our age could be less corrupt.

His words were icicle light,
Melting drops of green icicle light
That followed every butterfly
And dripped into rivulets whose arcana
The experienced boatman will never learn
Though he has fathomed
All the channels and deeps
Upon which he sails.

In all the frantically choreographed bustling,
The terrible hours will see the connections
Between obstacles and a battle of wits,
Between the search for truth
And the irony that undermining trials
Are more about the orderly search for truth
Than is finding a way through a thicket
Of the distinct and sharp reflections
Of options on the value of uncertainty
In the vicinity of the diffuse.

In the end, everything was hot as hell.

Welcome, Traveler

Welcome, traveler, to the cult
Of yet another cycle of damage
Crucial to embrace,
Free of familiar requirements.
Remember when you chased the dawn
By heading toward the dusk?
When the secrets of the hive
Would have been proud as,
Suddenly, you stood alone
To ambush a man who has no fear?

Nothing can invalidate the nearly completed phase
Of a sharing negotiated like a swashbuckling adventure.
There need not be a confrontation between land and sea.
Their influence on a man diffused, deformed,
Is compressed in sentiments that announce
The dynamics of a turbulent boundary
Where the source of all misfortune
Is also the source of hope.
The evidence you seek
Is proof of the generic model,
Of dynamic groups constructed
On theoretical schemes
Based on an approximation
Of a value that seems dependent
On an interest in gaining the expected.
Some would rather stare
Strangeness in the face.

I wanted my dream to become reality,
But reality became a dream
Where apologists for convictions
Based on faith alone

Are no better
No more truthful
No more worthy
Than random oracles
Or the predictions of failed time travelers
Who keep trying to return to the past
Only to show up late.
I'm waiting for a time
When the prosecution's star witness
Is an astronomer.

If reality is consensus-based,
Can there be a consensus of two?
Can there be consensus beyond our reach,
Beyond our ken?
And what of those overshadowed
By others greater in size, in power?
Where is that reality?
The problem with living on the high tower
Is that you cannot see what lies at your feet,
And life always erupts in relationships
Of interlocking processes, of exchanges,
Of sophistication, violence, and delights.

I have one small request
Before you expose yourself
To Medusa's deviant art:
Complete the cycle of damage
Before it gets worse,
Because if you create a niche,
A new predator will arise to fill it.

Elegy for Scott

"Sorry to leave such a mess," your note read.
"I just had to walk away.
I couldn't take the pain any more."

A true adherent
Of the law of conservation of energy,
You saw the horror
But filed it away for later.
You foresaw apocalypse,
But you filed it away
For a later that never came
And created your own apocalypse
Right in your own home.
Right in your own heart.
You only had one enemy in the world,
And he was yourself.

Were you crying?
Did you say something
To a world that never gave a shit
Before and now only could in the form
Of a 12-gauge?
"Fuck it," I hear you say
Since I've heard you say
It all too often—
Heard you say the world
Was too fucked up to give a shit about.
The problem is, if you don't give a shit
About the world, it doesn't give a shit
About you.
You have to believe and work toward a goal,
Even if it is a fantasy,
Because all else is darkness and despair.

I like to think life is a search for meaning,
But I guess you had about all the searching—
And meaning—you could take.

I cannot be rid of these demons
Constructed of the same stuff
As my brother's unrequited love.
And vengeful they are—
Wanting a life they cannot have
At a cost they would not be willing to pay.
My brother, you knew something of cost,
Didn't you, talking on the phone
From the midst of your darkness and squalor
As if it was just another day,
Another chance to get pissed or paranoid
Or go dumbass on some subject.
But I suppose I can't really blame you—
Or anyone else, either.
It's just the way things were.
We were all too young, too inexperienced,
Too ignorant, too unempowered,
And too caught up in circumstance.
What if there had been intervention?
But there wasn't, and now
All that is left are what ifs.

He told us he felt
Like he was always wearing a mask,
But it was more transparent than he realized
To those of us who knew him as well as anybody.
The last time I saw him, he was exhaustion
And pain, and beneath them,
The mask finally slipped, exposing a man
Haunted and defeated.
He looked old and shaken,
And he was smoking furiously,

As if an entire industry of self-destruction
Was down there inside him,
Churning on itself,
Burning itself out.
The next day, it was ash.

Life moves on
And eventually leaves
This frail flesh behind.
Who is terminally ill,
Physically or spiritually:
The ones who are dead and gone
Or the ones who are left behind?
Is your shade still here?
I sometimes believe I feel your presence.
Is it a mere shadow wrought by
Memory and loss, or is it really
You making things go bump?
If it's you, I hope you have good reason
To stick around
And aren't just stuck here
In a rut not much different
From the one you furrowed
Through the loam of life.
But if your shade is lurking about,
Hear this: I get pretty pissed
About it sometimes, you bastard.

Move on, dear brother.
There's a light out there,
And it has your name.

TEXAS WHITE LINE FEVER

Quick Change, Unexpected Beauty

When you drive long distances,
The terrain changes so gradually
Unfolding into different zones and climes.
People today are so used to quick change
That they want something to happen
Right now!
Right away!

Another little cross where somebody died,
Planted on a little knoll beside the road—
A white cutout
Marking a crucifixion of travel.
Imagine if the spirits of the dead
Must haunt these crosses,
These miniature crossroads
Of zone and clime.

Yes, change is usually slow on the road,
But sometimes it does come abruptly,
Like death or sudden,
Unexpected beauty.

Southeast Texas

Here is fertile soil.
Seems like almost anything can grow here—
Even a Vietnamese village.

Radio Towers

Familiar landmarks
Inhabiting hilltops
No matter where you go
Or where you've never been,
Marking legs of grids,
Casting overlapping spherical fields
Or projecting straight-line transmissions
Of information arcane
To the beasts of the landscapes
They stand above like skeletons
Of giants frozen in time.

The Highway Rural

The highway rural
Remembers the past
Within the present:
The white ranch fence,
The small terra cotta factory,
The rolled up hay bales,
The signs for the best eats in the county,
The bus stop shelters,
The farmhouse on the hill
With witch-hat façade
And western-gothic gateway—
Two skinned poles with a crosspiece.
Antiques litter the roadsides,
Some costing too much,
Some still in use,
Some just plain old junk.

Out in the open,
The traffic crawls between towns.
You can spot the locals,
Moving slowly but with certainty
In pickup trucks pulling trailers
Loaded with harrows,
Stock watering tanks,
And that ubiquitous country totem:
The deer blind on stilts
Looking like a short fire watchtower.
A watching firetower.

The banalities of the road
Are as hard pressed to define
As the mystical feeling

One gets traveling
These paths across the landscape,
Passing the occasional bicycle rider
All alone way out in the middle
Of nowhere.

183

Up here, it's long hills rolling
Like giant swells on an ocean
So frozen in time
That it has acquired a skin of grass
And sparse, scrubby trees.

You run such long distances without people
That passing anybody becomes an event.
You both wave, but danger resides
In those brief moments of discreet encounter
When you both relinquish a critical moment of control
To express your common humanity.

Little towns blink by bearing subliminal cultural messages:
Reduce Speed Ahead. Veterans of Foreign Wars Post.
County Civic Arena. Hunting and fishing licenses.
Wrought iron furniture painted white rusts on front porches.
I pass trains whose tracks run alongside the roads.
They are not slow freights, but I'm going faster.

Something is dead down there in Wildcat Creek.

Forgotten Road

Passing Forgotten Road,
Where red earth skims brown dirt
And vanishes in time and space
To let Texas limestone poke through;
Where the lonely corral sits empty
Because we've eaten its occupants;
Where you can smell the stockyard stink
Though you can't see a stockyard,
Though sight runs nearly to the horizon;
Where the rails run through it all.

There on a siding sits
An old caboose
Defunct, abandoned
To the sky—
As usual,
The very last car of its train.

I'm driving in front of a front:
The sky is dark in the mirror.

Cruise Control II

On the open road
We all consider each other erratic drivers.
But we're all on cruise control—
It's our vehicles, not us,
That are vying for speed and dominance.

Valleys

Driving a section of road that runs
Dead straight and true
Across a series of broad, shallow valleys
Dropping from the northern high plains
Southeastward to Central Texas.

Fooled by the clarity of distance
Out here where grass is king,
I think these valleys must be
Much narrower than they are,
But they clock in at fourteen miles across.

Occasional watercourses seam their broad expanses—
Some shallow, the larger eaten into deep gullies,
All lined by fingers of scrubby brush
Like the last faint tendrils of a dream
Clutching for remembrance of forests.

At last there comes a hill
High enough that the road
Must wind its way up in broad, sweeping arcs.
This hill bounds the last valley,
And from here on, water flows westward.

Across Mustang Creek

Across Mustang Creek, the land
Is one step toward the raw.
Everything is scrubbier, rougher—
Grasses, trees, cattle, towns.
The people.
Creosote-beam trestles suspend
The tracks of the ubiquitous railroad
That parallels the blacktop.
Pond dikes protrude rock rubble
Rounded like old bones laid long in the earth—
Bones of mountains whose shadows
Once walked this land.

A dead armadillo on the shoulder
Lies on its back, curled, semi-fetal,
A longneck Lonestar beer bottle
Clutched in its paws.
Dead drunk.

The irony—you hurtle along
And the scenery flashes by
And the terrain heaves and flattens
And the towns appear and vanish
And the waterways grow and diminish
And the weather marches across the landscape
And the wind blows new dust in through the windows,
But the metaphors of the road
Are so true and so unchanging
They become cliches.

I see a terrapin crossing the road.
A terrapin out here in the dust,

Where stream beds are becoming dry channels.
I stop and carry it to safety,
But it is a futile gesture.
For the next few miles,
There are so many terrapins crossing the road
That I'd have to walk the whole way
And have a strong back
For all the bending and scooping.
I can't be the terrapin god, saving one and all.
I have other tasks.
Besides, somebody else already is the terrapin god.

I come to a town,
Old, historic, stone buildings,
Once happening.
Now not large.
But the cemetery is large.
Very large.
The largest I've ever seen in a town this size.
Maybe the whole town is dying away.
Who will bury the last?

Certainty

In the cities
There are men and women
Who feel certain they have arrived.
Out in the desert,
The Earth isn't so self-assured.
Everything is unfinished,
As if all the workmen are on permanent break.
But out here, the workmen never cease—
The sun, the wind, the cold after dusk.
A sudden rain can change the landscape
Overnight.

The High Chaparral

On the high chaparral,
There's nothing for the wind to do
But blow and blow and blow.
It blows across the old ruins
And over the long, long trains.
It whips in weird currents
Around clusters of grain silos
The size of city blocks
That serve the huge farms
Spread across this huge land.
Even though it's Sunday,
Almost every farm
Has someone plowing the fields,
As if the work never ceases
For puny man
In this huge landscape.
Clouds massively splotch
Darkness across the gently rolling hills.
A hawk sits on a fencepost,
Watching the grasslands, the broad fields,
The rolling skyline miles and miles away
Beyond which the Earth either ends
Or stretches into eternity.
In a depression between two hills
Is a pond that will be dry by midsummer.

Seminole Canyon

Watching distant U.S. 90,
From a darkening wasteland above a canyon
Where shadowed petroglyphs
Shelter from the wash of constant winds
And tell indecipherable tales
Of a past beyond memory.
Headlights dip in and out of vales
And behind hills,
Migrating in pulses across
A darkness marked with memories
Of ancient seas.
What is the meaning
Of these new glyphs
Etched in substance
More ephemeral than memory?

In the fading western distance,
A train emerges from a darkened gap
And rounds a hill still lit by a sun
Certain only of its own passing.
And rounds it,
And rounds it.
How long can a train be?
Water may be scarce here,
But the land, winds, roads, and trains
Seem to go on forever,
As if they always have
And always will.

Ancient people left their marks
On the canyon walls, and we
Are permitted a glance.

Mess Box Creek

This land west of the Pecos
Is raw, is rocky, is dry,
Is barren and empty.
Is not devoid of spirit.
Names are important here,
Where people are as raw as the soil,
As sparse as this trickle
Called Mess Box Creek.

But this thin current
Has water enough for stock and men,
For the chuck wagon
That was heart as well as belly.
Simple names for literal men
Whose duration and numbers
Have not yet touched this country
With a patina of abstractions
That forget history,
That erase memory,
Though Indian names have vanished
With their namers.

I take a whiff, hoping
For the lingering scent of campfire,
But all that rises in the still heat
Is the faint odor of roadkill.
A small furry body lies on the pavement,
And about a hundred feet farther on
Flutters the body of a dead buzzard.
They say you are what you eat.

Light Is Sharp

Light is sharp.
Sound is mushier,
Always a few
Moments behind.

White Lines

The modern-day tumbleweed
Is the ubiquitous plastic bag.
I'm out in the middle of nowhere,
And for two miles before and after
Every crossroads store,
Plastic bags are blown against
The barbed wire fences
That line the roadsides,
Flapping like shredded
Pennants in the wind.

There are too many things to know.
We can only know a little bit about very little
And never even that about the ephemeral
Truths of wider spaces.
But there are things I do know for certain:
If you're walking, you're always one step behind;
Home is expected boundaries;
Light is that which goes faster than a thing can go;
Safer is an anagram of fears;
And we are all like barbed wire fences—
Grasping shreds of existence,
Wrapped in tatters of a dream.

Westward

1
Westward expansion across a remote
Prairie wilderness with no end,
Where huge piles and rolls of hay
Lie like giant dung on a landscape
That once was silt beneath a shallow sea
But now has gone from one extreme
Of humidity to another.
Here, you must heed those who recorded
The accepted way to cross the long, dry section
And heed the unmarked graves
At crossroads where direction of change
Is more important than change of direction.
Here, you must travel with purpose,
Though that purpose be hidden
Beyond the horizon.

2
Highways fly over the landscape,
But the smaller roads cling more closely
To the contours of the countryside,
To less-familiar amusements,
To treasures of pioneer history.
We are the living diaries
Of the people who traveled this way,
Just as we are those who travel in their footsteps.

3
Life is so literal out here
Where it clings to life beneath the constant wind,
Where windbreak trees surround the prairie houses,
Where the fields reach into eternity

And the largest hill is the curvature of the Earth.
Read the literal names:
Here's North Red Creek.
There was South Red Creek.
Way, way back, there was Red Creek.
Now there's Red Gully,
And nearby is the Red River.
The soil is red, rocky, raw.
Red like raw meat tingeing the water
With its blood, coloring human expression:
"Welcome to Robert Lee," the sign reads,
Letters red like raw meat on a black background.

4
A field to the right leads up a broad expanse
Ending in the sky.
Probably another valley beyond,
But it could be the end of the world.
I could drive up over that hill
And be gone forever.
A dirt road leads that way,
Luring fools like me
Who travel the world,
Sealing fate before disappearing
Like a bird's whistle
Gathered through an open window
Or drops of rain
That don't reach the ground.
Fading, fading, fading.

Phosphene Publishing Company
publishes books and DVDs relating to literature,
history, the paranormal, film, spirituality, and the
martial arts.

For other great titles, visit
phosphenepublishing.com

www.ingramcontent.com/pod-product-compliance
Lightning Source LLC
Chambersburg PA
CBHW061447040426
42450CB00007B/1263